THE DOLLAR ABROAD, INFLATION AT HOME

THE DOLLAR ABROAD, INFLATION AT HOME

John Charles Daly, *Moderator*

William Fellner
Robert Solomon
Herbert Stein
Henry Wallich

Held on August 31, 1978
and sponsored by
the American Enterprise Institute
for Public Policy Research
Washington, D.C.

This pamphlet contains the edited transcript of
one of a series of AEI forums.
These forums offer a medium for
informal exchanges of ideas on current policy problems
of national and international import.
As part of AEI's program of providing opportunities
for the presentation of competing views,
they serve to enhance the prospect
that decisions within our democracy will be based
on a more informed public opinion.
AEI forums are also available on
audio and color video cassettes.

AEI Forum 22

© 1978 by American Enterprise Institute
for Public Policy Research, Washington, D.C.
Permission to quote from
or reproduce materials in this publication is granted
when due acknowledgment is made.

ISBN 0-8447-2141-7
Library of Congress Catalog Card No. 78-57945

Printed in United States of America

JOHN CHARLES DALY, former ABC News executive and forum moderator: This Public Policy Forum, part of a series presented by the American Enterprise Institute, is concerned with the economic well-being of this nation at home and abroad. Our subject is, The Dollar Abroad, Inflation at Home.

Our dollar has been falling in value against other major currencies for a year. Now, bruised, battered, and sliding steeply to record lows, the declining dollar has taken center stage as one of the most urgent economic issues faced by the free world nations.

Foreign central banks, which bought $30 billion in 1977 to support the dollar against their currencies, have criticized the United States for its reluctance to intervene in the currency markets, on a large scale, to that same purpose. The administration's position has been that we support the present system of managed floating currencies, and that intervention should be used only to counter disorderly market conditions, not to establish, or peg, values at any particular level.

In the dog days of August 1978, the administration seems to have decided that disorderly market conditions have arrived. The White House announced that the sharp decline in the dollar and disorderly market conditions, at a time when the trade position is showing signs of real improvement, could threaten progress toward dealing with our inflation and achieving orderly growth at home and abroad.

Federal Reserve Board chairman William Miller and Secretary of the Treasury Michael Blumenthal were asked by the White House to consider what actions would be appropriate on their part, and to recommend presidential action to deal with this situation. The Fed and the Treasury moved promptly in the foreign currency and domestic credit markets, and increased gold sales.

The situation stabilized briefly, but the late August announcement that the U.S. trade deficit for July was just under $3 billion, the fourth largest monthly deficit ever, lost the ground gained by the administration's announced determination to strengthen the dollar.

For the average layman, all was confusion. What are the causes of the dollar's decline? What does it have to do with inflation at home? And what, if anything, can we do about it?

Dr. Stein, for five years you served as a member of the President's Council of Economic Advisers, and for three of those years as its chairman. Would you be good enough to explain in layman's terms why the dollar has steadily lost value around the world?

HERBERT STEIN, A. Willis Robertson professor of economics at the University of Virginia and AEI senior fellow: John, I don't know whether the question was meant to imply that the dollar has lost value because I was there for five years, but if that is the implication, I would like to deny it. [Laughter.] The dollar did decline somewhat while I was there, but that was only a correction of a great overvaluation of the dollar, which had been building up for a long time.

If you are asking why the dollar has declined more recently—that is, several years after I left the government—I think there are a number of reasons. There is something to the most common argument, which has often

2

been made by the administration, that the large imports of oil have something to do with it. We pay a great deal more to the oil-exporting countries than they spend here. I think our big balance of trade deficits with countries other than the oil-exporting countries also have something to do with it.

There are a number of reasons why people outside the United States, who have been holding an enormous part of their liquid assets in the form of dollars, would want to shift out of dollars and have a wider diversification of their assets, which would put some downward pressure on the dollar.

But while all of these factors and others would tend to explain why the dollar has gone down, I do not think any of them, or all of them together, would explain why the dollar has gone down as much as it has, without bringing in the fact that the United States has recently had more inflation than many of the other industrial countries. And there is a great suspicion, which is not without foundation, that we will go on having a higher inflation rate than the rest of the world. So if we project this kind of situation for five years, the U.S. price level may rise by that time to 30 percent more than the Swiss price level, or the German price level, or the Japanese price level. That has a large effect and is a crucial part of the explanation, because, according to the textbooks, we hold or value currencies for what they will buy. And we are seeing that the dollar will buy less than other currencies. So it has gone down.

MR. DALY: Dr. Wallich, you have served on the President's Council of Economic Advisers and now are a member of the Board of Governors of the Federal Reserve.

At the end of August, you warned that we may face an inflation rate of 8 percent through the end of 1979, which is considerably higher than the administration's official forecast. Does the dollar's loss of value play a major role in inflation at home?

3

HENRY WALLICH, member of the Board of Governors of the Federal Reserve System: The broad answer to that is yes. Let me make clear that I did not predict an 8 percent rate of inflation; I said that this might happen, and we need to take urgent action. It was part of a proposal I was making—to tax companies that give excessively high wage increases, and thereby help other measures we must take to restrain inflation.

The other measures we have to take are very familiar. We have to bring the budget deficit down and keep the money supply from growing excessively; these are essential things. My proposal for a tax on excessive wage increases is something that would also be helpful, but I do not expect it to be enacted very soon.

As far as the relationship of inflation and the dollar is concerned, I do see a two-way street. On one side, inflation causes our trade balance to deteriorate; it also causes people to take their money out of the United States. On the other side, the decline in the dollar that results from those events tends to accelerate our own inflation to some measurable degree.

MR. DALY: Dr. Fellner, after nearly forty years as professor of economics at the University of California, Berkeley, and at Yale, capped with service as a member of the President's Council of Economic Advisers, you are now directing a project on contemporary economic problems at the American Enterprise Institute. How do you rank the dollar crisis, if that is a proper description, among the current economic problems?

WILLIAM FELLNER, Sterling professor of economics emeritus at Yale University and AEI resident scholar: It is a very serious problem that is intimately connected with our domestic inflation problem.

4

In 1976, at a time when our inflation rate was coming down and our current account was approximately balanced, the dollar remained reasonably stable in the international markets. Then, in 1977, when our inflation rate was again accelerating, the valuation of the dollar in foreign markets declined sharply.

We do not know what the future will bring in this regard. So far, I do not see any firm anti-inflationary policy developing in this country. Nor do people in other countries see such a policy developing. This has a very large influence on the valuation of the dollar abroad.

The fact is that we had a very large deficit in our merchandise balance in 1977, as well as a very large deficit in our current account. And those deficits developed at a time when our inflation rate was accelerating.

There may be other reasons that are simply not captured in the price statistics, and they have to do with the improvements in the quality of traded goods of various countries. But what we call the inflation rate played a very large role in this, and I do not think that the dollar will recover, unless the foreign markets see us develop a firm policy to get our inflation rate down.

MR. DALY: Dr. Solomon, you served with the Federal Reserve Board for nearly thirty years, focusing particularly on international finance, and as a senior fellow at the Brookings Institution, you are now exploring the relationship between the exchange-rate system and world inflation. What are the bases of that relationship?

ROBERT SOLOMON, senior fellow at the Brookings Institution: Let me introduce a little diversity, if I may, by differing slightly with what some of my colleagues have been saying. I would like to approach the subject from a different angle and say that what has been called the dollar problem can also be looked upon as a problem of the rising value of three other currencies: the German mark, the Swiss franc, and the Japanese yen. Those are not the only currencies that have gone up, but they are the ones that have gone up most. When we speak of the falling dollar, we mean that the dollar has lost value in relation to those currencies, which we can also describe as an increase in their value.

In my view, this change in exchange rates, however we describe it, is not only the result of the acceleration of inflation in the United States—which I take as seriously as my colleagues do—but also a result of what has been happening in those three countries. And that has not been mentioned yet; I'm sure it will come up as our discussion goes along.

So I would simply like to broaden our topic and say that the economic stagnation in Europe and very slow expansion in Japan have a lot to do with the movement of exchange rates, which we've been calling the fall of the dollar.

DR. FELLNER: May I ask a question here? I do not think the markets anticipate a continuation of these growth rate differentials, because we have not had a record of growing more rapidly than those other countries, and I do not think anybody expects us to grow more rapidly. Indeed, if this were the expectation, it would have provided substantial incentives for investing capital in the United States during 1977.

The reason why that incentive has not developed is that nobody really expected these growth rate differentials to continue. Our growth rate was considered to be an unsound, inflationary growth rate that would prevail temporarily. Other countries were considered sounder, in that they paid a price for a healthier future growth development.

Therefore, if the markets valued the dollar as they did in 1977, it was not a consequence of anybody's believing that these growth rate differentials would continue, but rather a consequence of the fact that these growth rates were associated with the flare-up of inflation in the United States. The much more moderate growth rates of the other countries were interpreted as clearing the ground for future healthy growth.

This leads me back to the assumption that inflation has played the dominant role here, because what people feel might continue is the inflation differential, not the growth rate differential.

DR. SOLOMON: Is that a question? [Laughter.]

DR. WALLICH: I think you might give us a little more credit for good performance, Dr. Fellner. We have had a good expansion that has lasted a long time, and we have come to full employment. At full employment, we buy a lot. Other countries are far from full employment. Since they are lagging, they buy little from us, and that has given us a big deficit.

MR. DALY: You have used the phrase "full employment," Dr. Wallich, and some of us who are not economists want to know more about unemployment rates. Would you describe why you called it "full employment"?

DR. WALLICH: I would say that somewhere in the range of 5½ to 6 percent unemployment, we have a condition where we can not expand further without generating inflationary pressure, and that is what I call full employment. We are not exactly at it, but we are very close to it. And under those conditions, if the rest of the world is not at full employment, we naturally develop a trade deficit. I would say that maybe $10, $15, or even $20 billion of our trade deficit is due simply to this difference in the phase of the business cycle here and abroad. And that has certainly hurt the dollar.

DR. STEIN: But the question is why a trade deficit of $15 or $20 billion, if it was believed to have resulted from something as certainly temporary as the divergence in the growth rates, should have had such a large effect on the dollar. After all, the rest of the world is holding hundreds of billions of dollars. How much decline of the dollar is required to make them willing to hold another $15 or $20 billion worth?

It seems to me that if there was confidence that our inflation rate would not exceed that of other countries, and that this divergence of the growth rates would be temporary, it would have taken only a very small decline of the dollar to induce people to hold the dollars that were generated by our trade deficits and current account deficits. So I think the trade deficit contributed something, but it is hard to explain declines of the magnitude we've had by that factor.

DR. SOLOMON: May I respond to the question that both Dr. Fellner and Dr. Stein have posed?

MR. DALY: Would you begin your response by differentiating between the trade account and the current account?

DR. SOLOMON: Well, the so-called trade account is simply the result of our merchandise imports and exports. Our merchandise imports have been exceeding our merchandise exports; therefore, we have what is called a trade deficit.

The current account position, which is also in deficit, includes our receipts from travel abroad, our expenditures for travel abroad, our receipts from U.S. investments abroad, and our payments for foreign investments in the United States—so-called invisible items in the balance of payment.

I would like to make a couple of points in response to the questions that were put.

It may well be that the public expected the difference in growth rates to continue for some time. I do not know whether the public fully appreciated how stagnant the economies of Europe were. But we all know that, despite the stagnation, the head of the German government, like the leaders of other European countries, again and again stressed that he did not intend to take stimulative actions recommended by people on the other side of the Atlantic—that is, the United States. He had his own good reasons for making those statements; he is concerned about inflation.

Those who are forming expectations about the future may expect that the European economy will remain sluggish and stagnant for some considerable period of time. They do not regard this difference in growth rates as being quite as temporary as Dr. Fellner and Dr. Stein may believe.

DR. WALLICH: I suspect that technicalities, like differences in growth rates, are not the primary thing that the market perceives, although they surely are perceived. And I do not know what market expectations are, but in every discussion of the dollar in the newspapers, foreign exchange traders talk about the deficit. And it has to be explained that the deficit is partly temporary because of this cyclical divergence of our growth rates. And there are other factors, like the oil situation. Behind it all lies inflation, which gets us back to our topic.

DR. SOLOMON: But inflation does not lie behind the oil deficit. Another reason why I think my colleagues are putting excessive emphasis on inflation as an explanation for the exchange-rate movement is that in late 1977 and early 1978 most of the talk in the newspapers, which was attempting to explain the fall in the dollar or the rise in the other currencies, focused on our excessive oil imports.

To my knowledge, no one has said that we import oil excessively because of inflation. That is quite a separate factor. So there is at least one other consideration besides inflation to explain the exchange-rate movement.

DR. STEIN: Of course, it is unwise to rely on the newspapers for explanations of why things happen. [Laughter.]

DR. SOLOMON: But we're talking about market expectations, which, presumably, are formed partly in that way.

DR. STEIN: It is interesting that the biggest decline of the dollar has come during the period in which the oil deficit has been declining. The oil deficit has been declining since the first or second quarter of 1977.

DR. SOLOMON: 1978.

DR. STEIN: No, our trade deficit with the OPEC countries has declined since the second quarter of 1977, quarter by quarter.

And, of course, it is quite natural that the administration—of which none of us is a member—should have attributed the decline of the dollar to the energy problem and the oil problem. Every administration for the last twenty years has attributed the decline of the dollar, or the problem of the dollar, to the failure to enact some policy that it was pushing. That's the way Lyndon Johnson got the tax surcharge through, by saying that if it wasn't passed, the dollar would decline. That has been going on for a long time. It is a way to frighten the American people into doing something the administration wants done, by raising the scarecrow that if they don't do it, the dollar will go down.

And there are lots of good reasons why the Europeans should also focus attention on the energy problem; it diverts attention from them. After all, when we first had the energy problem and began to run the big deficits with the OPEC countries, the dollar went up. There was a lot of explanation and very good reasoning behind the idea that the oil situation would make the dollar go up, and that is what it did.

DR. SOLOMON: Dr. Fellner put us on the track of talking about what people expect, and I think this has led us to say some things that we ourselves may not believe. We are trying to explain peoples' expectations about exchange rates, because those expectations have been influencing exchange rates.

DR. WALLICH: The psychology of the falling dollar.

DR. SOLOMON: Right.

DR. FELLNER: Yes, but if people had expected growth rate differentials to continue—those growth rate differentials favoring the United States that we observed in 1977—there would have been a very large incentive for capital to move into the United States.

DR. SOLOMON: Well, direct investment did move into the United States.

DR. FELLNER: On a very small scale. On the whole, the balance of private capital movements was strongly negative in 1977.

DR. SOLOMON: That's right—again, because of those same expectations.

DR. FELLNER: I don't think people really expected the American growth rate to be permanently and soundly higher than that of the rival countries. They expected the differential to be a temporary one that would not induce any substantial capital movements into the United States.

DR. WALLICH: I think people abroad regard the United States as a good place to invest, Dr. Fellner. They say everything is cheap here, which cannot be denied if you look at the rate of the Swiss franc, the D-mark, and the yen. This is a country with political stability, giving assurance of continuity in the investment climate, and a lot of money has been coming in.

What we have observed in outflow of capital is, in good part, a result of the fact that the central banks have bought dollars; that is, they have moved money into the United States. And when money is moved into one place, other money tends to flow out. Many of the private capital outflows that we had in 1977 occurred because foreign central banks intervened in the markets by buying dollars, thus pushing money into the United States.

MR. DALY: Can I bring us all back to what has happened in these first seven months of 1978?

Following the White House call for action in August, the Fed and the Treasury moved on a broad front to correct the fall of the dollar. There is, of course, a broad public relations drive that hopes to persuade the international financial markets that the dollar is stronger than it looks, and that it will soon be on the road to recovery.

But what are the reasons for the more specific moves, and what results are hoped for? Did the Fed intervene on a substantial scale in the exchange markets? What did it do, and is it working? Dr. Wallich?

DR. WALLICH: I suppose I'm on the spot there. We report on our intervention with a certain time-lag, and indeed, whenever there have been disorderly markets, the Fed has intervened.

There is a belief that all we have to do is to intervene in the market, that is, buy dollars and sell D-marks, and the dollar will stabilize. Well, that is not so. There are hundreds of billions of dollars that can move. But if the market believes that the rate will go one way, and the central bank tries not to let it, the market will overrule the central bank because it has so much more money.

So the question isn't really whether, by exchange-market intervention, one should try to change the course of events and the rate of the dollar in particular; it's simply that one cannot have more than a small influence. That influence is best exerted if one tries to keep the exchange market orderly, but otherwise lets the fundamentals of the situation—including inflation, unfortunately—work themselves out.

DR. STEIN: The most fundamental development that has occurred in policy to support the dollar has been the administration's support, however tacit or passive, of the Federal Reserve's policy of tightening money and allowing interest rates to rise. It is significant that when the Federal Reserve raised the discount rate, the administration said that it fully understood why the Federal Reserve did so.

MR. DALY: Would you define the discount rate for us?

DR. STEIN: The Federal Reserve discount rate is the rate at which the Federal Reserve banks will lend to their member banks. The member banks come to borrow when they are short on reserves, when they want to extend more credit and do not have the basis for doing so. By raising the discount rate, the Federal Reserve makes it a little more expensive for them, and they tend not to do it so much. Anyway, in the financial community it is regarded as a signal of tightness.

Previously, there had been a feeling around the country, and perhaps the world, that the administration was very reluctant to see money tightened and to see interest rates rise. There had been a lot of grumbling from various administration officials about it. And this led to doubts, here and abroad, about whether the Federal Reserve would be able to carry out an anti-inflationary policy, especially one that involved higher interest rates. Now that doubt has been removed somewhat, although not conclusively in my opinion. Nevertheless, I think it was a good thing to have happened.

MR. DALY: All right, the federal funds rate target was also raised. Would one of you please tell the members of our audience—who may have read about this in the paper—what the federal funds rate target is and what it is supposed to do?

DR. WALLICH: As you know, the Federal Reserve tries to regulate the growth of the money supply. This is done by changing one interest rate—the rate at which banks borrow and lend to each other what surplus funds they have. By changing that rate slightly, we can influence this interbank borrowing and lending, and therefore the banks' willingness to lend to customers and thereby expand the money supply. The federal funds rate, thus, is a means of regulating the growth of the money supply.

MR. DALY: Monthly gold sales will increase materially in November from 300,000 ounces a month to 750,000 ounces. Is the sale of gold wise? If so, is it productive in a dollar crisis, Dr. Fellner?

14

DR. FELLNER: I think the sale of gold falls in the category of operations which Dr. Wallich described a moment ago. In other words, it is essentially a support operation. It is an intervention in favor of the dollar, meant to strengthen the dollar. I do not expect very much yield from that kind of operation, and I think the basic problem there is getting the inflation rate down gradually. If that is done in a credible fashion, I think the dollar will recover; if not, I do not think the dollar's recovery will come simply from these support operations.

DR. WALLICH: Without disagreeing on the fundamental importance of inflation, Dr. Fellner, I think you might give the Treasury a little more credit for its gold operation. In addition to its being an intervention-type operation, it also means a substantial reduction in our net gold imports. When we import gold, we put dollars out into the world, just as we do when we import cars or televisions. Sale of Treasury gold can offset some $1.5–2 billion in gold imports, which is a substantial improvement in our trade account. And it has a strong psychological effect on foreigners, who are really not convinced that the United States wants to see its currency strong. No matter what we say or do, the rumor abroad is that the United States wants the dollar down.

When we take an action that involves giving up some of our reserve assets, it carries a lot of conviction.

DR. STEIN: Do you think it important for us to correct this mistaken perception of our views, if it is a mistaken perception? I was impressed with something Mr. Daly said earlier about the dollar being "bruised and battered." That figure of speech is commonly used in these discussions, and it suggests that the dollar really ought to be standing up straight as a ramrod, and that something terrible has happened if it is bruised and battered. Other people might say that the dollar is just swimming about gracefully, like a fish in a pond, and though for the moment it is declining, at some time it will rise. So why be concerned about it?

DR. SOLOMON: I tried to say something like that at the beginning, but I didn't say it as gracefully as you just did, Dr. Stein.

DR. STEIN: I think it is a good question for us to discuss. I was particularly struck by that phrase, "bruised and battered," because I read in a news magazine that the Americans in Europe were "battered" by the decline of the dollar. I read it on a plane while returning from France, where I had spent two weeks. During that time, the dollar had fallen 2.2 percent against the franc, and I calculated that the cost of that was about the equivalent of one medium-priced lunch. So I didn't feel battered by it at all. And it is not at all clear that we need to feel greatly concerned about this.

Dr. Wallich said that the decline of the dollar is inflationary. That is a common statement, and maybe there is a lot to it. But it always puzzles me, because, if we generated the decline of the dollar by our own inflation, until the dollar does decline we have really just put off on the rest of the world some of the inflationary consequences of our own inflation. When the dollar declines, then those inflationary consequences come back home to us. It is not because the dollar declined that we have inflation; it is because we did things that were inflationary. We can pawn that off on other people for a while, by getting them to sell us stuff cheap, but after a while they won't.

DR. SOLOMON: Well, there is another side to this, and I hope it is not too technical. But one can make the same point Dr. Stein just made from the point of view of the European countries. Consider Germany, for instance. By operating its economy at much too low a level and holding its industrial production virtually unchanged for a year and a half while its exports went up, Germany experienced an appreciation of its currency, which in turn reduced the cost (in D-marks) of its imports and helped to bring about a lower rate of inflation in Germany.

The lower rate of inflation abroad, particularly in the three countries mentioned earlier, is partly a result of the fact that their exchange rates have gone up. So in a sense, by first operating their economies at too stagnant a condition, they have exported inflation to the rest of us, making our currencies go down in relation to their currencies and making the cost of our imports go up.

The point is not often stated that way, but I did so to give the counterpart of what Herb Stein just said. While he may believe that the United States has exported inflation to other countries, I believe that Germany has exported inflation, or achieved its own low rate of inflation at the expense of other countries.

DR. WALLICH: Well, I wouldn't wish inflation on anybody, and I would not argue that a country ought to inflate in order to get out of that bind, but I think there is something to what Dr. Solomon says. The countries with strong currencies have had cheaper imports, and that has helped them to bring down their inflation. I suppose that is a testimonial to the success of their policies.

So it still comes down to the question, How do we get rid of our own inflation, despite the fact that the dollar has declined, thereby making it harder? As we succeed in answering that, the dollar will, of course, respond favorably.

DR. FELLNER: May I very briefly come back to one question? Dr. Stein asked why it really matters whether or not an exchange rate goes down.

If there were very regular differentials in exchange rates year after year, the markets could predict them and could gear their activities to them. That might describe an equilibrium condition. I think it is inconceivable that equilibrium would develop in response to the differentials between inflation rates which we now see. We observed in 1977 that things were quite unpredictable. The markets were in great uncertainty, and that must have had an adverse influence on their activities. And there continues to be uncertainty as to what these inflation rates and exchange rates will be even next month. This uncertainty can become very damaging to world trade and to the activities in the various economies. So it is the unpredictability, rather than the existence, of the differential that—

DR. STEIN: So that is a reason for being concerned about a rapid, erratic, and unforeseen decline, as compared with some other kind of decline, if some other kind is conceivable. Nevertheless, while the uncertainty must increase the cost of doing business in some way and must impair efficiency, I don't know whether anybody, looking at things from an international perspective, has seen the damaging consequences of that. Is trade growing less rapidly than was expected?

DR. SOLOMON: It is growing less rapidly, but for other reasons.

DR. STEIN: Yes, but can you attribute any of it to this uncertainty factor?

DR. WALLICH: It's probably growing more slowly than it would otherwise.

DR. STEIN: Does it manifest itself as something more than an increase in the cost of ship insurance, or something like that?

DR. SOLOMON: You are asking a good question, Dr. Stein. I doubt that any of us at this table can answer it, but it is a question well worth asking.

MR. DALY: Then let me move to a few more technical things that the general public reads about, but may not quite understand.

Reading the story of the fall of the dollar, we learn of proposals that might be used by the Fed, the Treasury, or the administration: proposals about borrowing foreign exchange from the international monetary fund, about using our special drawing rights, and about something called "swap lines."

Would someone define those three elements and tell us whether or not there is any substantial reason to think they can relieve the pressure on the dollar?

DR. SOLOMON: I think Henry Wallich has already answered that question, but let me quickly go over what is involved in the proposals you have just referred to. By any of the three methods—(1) using its right to borrow from the international monetary fund, (2) using the special drawing right, or (3) using lines of credit that the Federal Reserve has with other central banks—the United States could borrow or get hold of additional amounts of foreign currencies. Selling those in the market would tend to prop up the dollar. By absorbing dollars, we would be increasing the supply of other currencies and reducing the supply of dollars in markets. That is the purpose of those proposals.

But, as Henry Wallich has already said, the amounts of dollars and other currencies held in the world are very large, and as our many, many years of fixed exchange rates under the Bretton Woods system have shown, it is not possible for the monetary authorities to stand up against a market that believes an exchange rate will move.

So I doubt very much that the proposals I have just tried to describe will do very much to solve what we have been calling "the dollar problem," which, again, could also be thought of as a German mark problem, a Japanese yen problem, or a Swiss franc problem.

MR. DALY: One school of thought suggests that speculation is probably playing a large part in what is happening to the dollar, and that we should have free-floating exchange rates. Supposedly, if we have free-floating exchange rates, the speculators will get out because speculating will become too risky. Do you find any particular worth in the concept of free-floating exchange rates, as against the managed float we have now?

DR. SOLOMON: I think the float has been managed rather lightly, actually, which is consistent with what Henry Wallich has said. So for the most part, speculators have to take their chances against what they think other private individuals will do, and only occasionally do they have to contend with the possibility that a central bank will step into the market. I do not think we are all that far from a free float. The speculators do not have a free ride.

DR. FELLNER: May I ask Dr. Solomon and Dr. Wallich a question? Were those interventions in 1977 really so small? I would deduct the OPEC part from the $30 billion, because maybe it's market-oriented, even if it is—

DR. SOLOMON: You might also deduct the one-time movement into the pound sterling, which was certainly not designed to prop up the dollar.

DR. FELLNER: No, but it was designed to prevent sterling from rising.

DR. SOLOMON: Right.

MR. DALY: Please, I can hardly handle the dollar. Let's leave sterling out. [Laughter.]

DR. SOLOMON: You're a sterling fellow, John. [Laughter.]

DR. FELLNER: But what is the difference between preventing sterling from rising and preventing the dollar from falling?

DR. SOLOMON: The fact that sterling was rising against all currencies, not just the dollar. There is a difference.

DR. FELLNER: Well, yes, it was rising against many currencies. Nevertheless, even if we deduct that, there remain rather substantial interventions in 1977. And what about the first quarter of 1978? There seems to have been very substantial interventions, in excess of $10 billion, in that quarter.

What is substantial is a relative concept, I will admit, but I wouldn't say that those interventions could be called small.

DR. WALLICH: Evidently, they were nowhere near large enough to prevent the movement on the exchange rate.

DR. FELLNER: That is absolutely correct.

DR. SOLOMON: Let me introduce one further factor which hasn't come up yet. Between March and June or early July of 1978, the exchange rate between the dollar and the European currencies was virtually stable; it hardly moved at all.

There may have been some ups and downs, but there was very little net movement. Now, the yen did continue to move up against the dollar, and against other currencies as well. But there was a period of three months of stability, and it was during that period when inflation seemed to be accelerating in the United States.

This is a fact that I think my friends Dr. Stein and Dr. Fellner ought to digest and bring into their thoughts.

DR. STEIN: My interpretation of that period was exactly the opposite of yours. In that period, it seemed to me that despite the very high inflation rates that were heavily influenced by food, there was, for the first time in six or nine months, some glimmer of hope that we would get the inflation rate down. It was the time of Mr. Carter's April 11th speech, in which he said that inflation was his first priority, and that we would have a new national program to fight it. It was the time that the public became convinced that Mr. Miller, the new chairman of the Federal Reserve, was firmly devoted to fighting inflation. And the stock markets and money markets at home also reflected the hope that this surge of inflation would, indeed, prove to be temporary, and that we were finally on our way towards a more anti-inflationary policy.

And the renewal of the decline of the dollar coincided with the waning of that hope, which was partly caused by the evidence that Mr. Carter's anti-inflation program was not working, that the incomes policy did not amount to anything. It was also caused by new questions about the intentions of the Federal Reserve that were precipitated by some statements and actions of the chairman.

So if you look, not at the current inflation rate for that period, but at the prevailing expectations, which can be judged intuitively by examining one's own expectations and assuming that other people share them, the expectations about inflation corresponded closely to the movement of the exchange rate.

DR. SOLOMON: Let me present an alternative explanation. (After all, when four economists get together, they come up with at least five different views.)

It just so happens that, during the fourth quarter of 1977 and into January 1978, the German economy accelerated after a period of stagnation. And two months after that the dollar stabilized. The Japanese economy began to expand as well in the late fall of 1977, and it continued expanding rapidly into the spring of this year.

I believe those two facts—the apparent speedup in economic activity and therefore imports into Europe and Japan—had something to do with the stabilization of the exchange rate in the spring of 1978.

Now, in June, German industrial production fell, and the expansion of the Japanese economy seemed to have stopped and reversed itself. Once again, I would attribute this move in exchange rates partly to the developments within those economies.

DR. STEIN: Well, Mr. Daly, I think we know everything except two things: why the dollar went down, and whether it makes any difference that it did. So, maybe we should explain to you how to stop it. [Laughter.]

MR. DALY: I have heard that there are 400 or 500 billion American dollars in foreign hands. Is that correct? And, if so, isn't it one of our basic problems that there are so many dollars outside the country, in the hands of people whom we cannot influence, in terms of how to use it?

DR. WALLICH: I think that is a scare number which we should not be very concerned about.

DR. SOLOMON: Agreed.

DR. WALLICH: And it includes a great deal of double counting. One bank in London deposits dollars in another bank, which deposits the dollars in still another bank. Each bank makes an eighth of 1 percent by doing so, and the same dollars are counted more than once.

Nevertheless, the amount of dollars outside the United States is very large. But remember that the dollars in our country count, too—a person can take his money abroad, if he feels sufficiently concerned. So it does not really matter whether there are dollars outside or dollars here as long as we have free capital movements, and those cannot be changed. The world is much too integrated to do anything about that. As long as capital can move freely, there will be very large movements. And the only way to prevent adverse movements is to create an environment in which people have confidence in the currency and country that they have their money in. That's what we have to address ourselves to.

MR. DALY: So again we come back to expectations. After listening to this learned argument with much fascination, I would say there is general agreement that inflation at home does have an impact—whether great or minor—on the dollar and where it stands.

One other area that we have touched upon only indirectly through our discussion of inflation is the federal budget deficit. There is a school of thought that claims a drastic reduction in our federal budget deficit would have a beneficial effect on people's expectations, which you gentlemen find so very important to the picture. I wonder what we can do to reduce the federal budget deficit. Is this the one route above all others that must be travelled in order to fight inflation?

DR. WALLICH: It is essential, but it is not the only route. We are almost at full employment in this country, and we still have a very large budget deficit. In the old days, we used to say that at full employment, we should have a surplus. Now, though, we're not talking about a surplus, or even about getting to balance very quickly. We will in time, I hope.

To have a large deficit at this stage of the business cycle is pretty troublesome; we have made considerable headway, however, in bringing down the expected deficit for 1979.

DR. SOLOMON: I might say one thing, not necessarily in defense of budget deficits, but in explanation of at least a part of the budget deficit that we have even though we are near full employment. Two important facts should be mentioned.

First, our state and local governments have a surplus of some $30 billion, which is unusual; and second, as we've already said, our balance of payments has a current account deficit somewhere in the vicinity of $18–20 billion.

It is desirable that that balance of payments deficit be reduced, and as it is reduced, there should be a corresponding reduction in the federal budget deficit. But as long as we have that balance of payments deficit and that large surplus in the state and local governments, it makes sense to have a larger federal budget deficit than we would have normally. That doesn't mean that every dollar of the deficit is justified or that the deficit should not go down, but it explains why the deficit is larger now, as we approach full employment, than it has been in the past.

DR. STEIN: Or one could say the reverse, that as long as we have this big budget deficit, we will have the deficit in our international accounts, because the budget deficit—

DR. SOLOMON: You can't really—

DR. STEIN: —pumps up the U.S. economy, and makes us suck in all these imports—

DR. SOLOMON: But you don't really believe that, Herb.

DR. STEIN: I believe that getting the budget deficit down is part of this process of getting down the rate of inflation, and getting down the rate of inflation in this country is a way of correcting both the dollar position and the balance of payments position.

And there is another possible use for all those savings. Private investment might expand if the budget were not absorbing so much.

The key question is whether or not the U.S. economy is being subjected to excess demand.

DR. SOLOMON: Do you believe it is today?

DR. STEIN: Yes, I think it is. I think it has been for a year.

DR. SOLOMON: Then I think we have a basic difference of view there.

MR. DALY: When you say "excess demand," do you mean demand from the public for goods and services?

DR. STEIN: Demand from everybody for goods and services.

DR. SOLOMON: I think this is one basic difference between us.

DR. STEIN: Sure.

DR. FELLNER: Excess demand can be satisfied only by misleading people as to what their real incomes will turn out to be. That is to say, demand will lead to an unanticipated rise in prices, and thus lead people to do things for which they won't earn the real incomes they were expecting. That is, I think, a situation into which we have, indeed, arrived.

Dr. Wallich: Look at the data. The economy and manufacturing are operating at about 84 percent of capacity. But that doesn't mean that we have to go up to 100 percent. Historically, we have gotten some impression of shortages, some pressures on capacity, in the range of 87-88 percent, and there are always some lines, like cement, right now, in which there are significant shortages, even though other industries are not yet at that level.

Mr. Daly: There is a theory that our economy is beginning to cool off a bit. Perhaps that will help us with the general problem we have discussed this evening.

This concludes another Public Policy Forum, presented by the American Enterprise Institute for Public Policy Research. On behalf of AEI, our heartfelt thanks to the distinguished panelists, Dr. William Fellner, Dr. Robert Solomon, Dr. Herbert Stein, and Dr. Henry Wallich, for their participation.

THE U.S. POSTAL SYSTEM: CAN IT DELIVER?